Nature's Verses

Voices From the Earth and Her Solar Family

ROBERT PERRY

Acknowledgements

I wish to express my deep gratitude to the late Bob Tolz of the Cafh Foundation for his consistent kindness, encouragement and good cheer when the idea of pulling together a poetry collection based on communications with the natural world first came to me nearly two decades ago. In the same way, Dr. Richard Ackerman, Dr. Peter Cohen and Dr. Robert Magrisso offered encouraging commentary on a good number of the poems and I thank them very much.

Rose McHale and Dean Elder were absolutely essential in getting the manuscript into a form that might look publishable. Their generosity and whole-hearted backing of this work has been unequivocal and I thank them both deeply. And all during the many years that poems were being gathered, Nancy Conklin, Kathy Crawford, and Jonah and Wes Wittkamper offered encouragement for this undertaking. My brother Jesse Perry, and his partner Becky also expressed heart-felt optimism regarding the outcome of this work. It was Jesse who long ago introduced me to the natural world through his encyclopedic knowledge and tremendous enthusiasm regarding the natural world. And my sister, Sarah Perry — because of her unparalleled enthusiasm

4

4

and understanding of the poems —helped to push this effort over the finish line with a thousand gentle shoves from her heart.

In addition, Scott and Hella McVay engaged with a sampling of these poems and encouraged me to continue. Wes Jackson of The Land Institute inspired me very early on with his straightforward embrace of the Earth as a living planet. And finally, the indigenous peoples I met in Manaus, Brazil understood both the seriousness and timeliness of this work. Their recognition of the need for larger numbers of human beings to hear directly from the natural world was clear and tremendously empowering.

Lastly, I thank the Divine Mother, the Eternal Presence (or whatever you wish to call Her) for remaining at the center of my being for the whole of my lifetime, whether I acknowledged Her or not. And in the same way, I am most grateful to Gaia, our living Earth, for sustaining me and the countless forms of life with which I am delighted and honored to share space, time and experiences.

Dedication

This book of devic poetry is dedicated to:
Kathy, **Wesley**, **Jonah**, **Lis**, **Akira** *and* **Sky**

And to
Lightworkers everywhere, but especially
Janice, **Tom**, **Cathie**, **Barb**, **Sarah**, **Rose** *and* **Dean**

Introduction
Listening to the Living World

There is a language older than words. It is spoken in the rustle of leaves, the hush of snowfall, the low hum of whales beneath the ocean's liquid skin. It pulses in the veins of trees and glimmers in the eyes of foxes and frogs. It is the language of life itself—of Earth communicating her consciousness, intelligence and sensitivity through her many forms. This book is an invitation to listen.

The poems that follow are not authored in the usual sense. They are transmissions— words from the devas (a Sanskrit word which translates as "radiant," "shining one," "divine being") of plants, animals, minerals, and planets. They are the voices of beings who have long watched humanity with wonder, sorrow, and hope. Some speak with the patience of stone, others with the urgency of beating hearts. Some sing in the rhythm of tides, others murmur in the stillness of moss. All speak with the desire to be heard—not for their own sake alone, but for the sake of the vast network of life. And all express their concern and love for humanity as a species of wondrous capacity and potential.

We live in a time of great forgetting. The forests are disappearing, the oceans warming, the skies thick with the breath of machines. Species vanish like dreams upon waking. Rivers are dammed, mountains mined, soil poisoned. And yet, amid this unraveling, there is a deeper crisis: the loss of relationship. Living with its extractive mind-set, much of humanity has turned away from its kin—the more-than-human world—and in doing so, has turned away from itself.

This book is a gesture of remembrance. It seeks to restore the sacred conversation between humans and the rest of creation. It asks: What might we learn if we listened to the Earth not as a resource, but as a cherished companion? What wisdom might emerge if we allowed the oak to speak, the fox to counsel, diatoms to sing? What healing might begin if we recognized that the planet is not merely our home, but our teacher, our mirror, our sustainer and soul-mate?

The poems herein are not sentimental. They do not flatter. They speak with clarity and conviction, sometimes with grief, sometimes with fierce love. A tropical tree may lament its falling body. Bees may plead for the flowers they no longer find. Our farthest planet may offer perspective from the edge of our solar family. These voices rarely scold—they beckon. They ask us to remember our place in the great lattice of life, not as dominators, but as participants and co-creators.

Each poem is a portal. Through it, you may enter the consciousness of another being. You may feel the pulse of chlorophyll, the ache of migration, the joy of pollination. You may glimpse the world through eyes not your own—and in doing so, expand your sense of self. To listen deeply is to be changed. To hear the Earth is to become more human.

This is not a book of fantasy. It is a book of understandings as felt by the living world. The spirits who speak here are real, though not always visible. They dwell in the liminal spaces: between root and soil, between breath and wind, between dream and waking. They are the animating, energetic forces behind form. They are the soul of nature, and they are calling.

Their collective request is simple: Extend your compassion. Widen your circle of concern. Let your empathy reach beyond the human to embrace all beings. Try not to limit your caring to your children alone, but for the children of narwhals, of box turtles, of mahogany trees. Try not to limit your concern to your personal future, but to the future of coral reefs and cloud forests. Expand your attention beyond your own concerns and suffering to the lives of rivers and rainforests. Let your love be planetary.

This is not a burden—it is a blessing. To care deeply is to live fully. To recognize the sensitivities of the natural world is to grasp the very real connection between that world and humanity. To experience the losses of the world is to feel its beauty more vividly. To grieve the loss of a species is to honor its existence. To act on behalf of the Earth is to reclaim your own soul. Compassion is not weakness—it is strength. It is the force that binds galaxies and germinates seeds. It is the heartbeat of evolution.

The spirits who speak in this book do not ask for perfection. They ask for presence. They ask for humility, for curiosity, for courage. They ask you to walk gently, to listen deeply, to act wisely. They ask you to remember that you are not alone—that you are part of a vast, sentient community. They ask you to become a steward, a poet, a healer.

And so, let this book be a beginning. Let it be a doorway into deeper listening. Let it awaken your senses, stir your conscience, ignite your imagination. Let it remind you that the Earth and her sister planets are alive. Let it guide you toward a more compassionate way of being, one rooted in reverence and reciprocity.

May you hear the song of the stars in the silence of night. May you feel the wisdom of the wind in your lungs. May you see the sacred in the soil beneath your feet. May you know that every leaf, every feather, every stone has a story—and that you are part of it.

Welcome to the conversation. The Earth's voices are familiar to indigenous peoples around the world. Will you join them in listening?

–Robert Perry
September, 2025

Table of Contents

Deva of the Wren
(*Thryothorus ludovicianus*)
5/10/14

Introduction:
O assembled beings of wonder and light of sea-salt fluid
all tubular-held up by facsimile of stone: bone, tendon and ligament-
peace to you and yours the world over. Troubled are some of you
and wholly unaware of your sacredness. Our poem is thus, sung out
as only our feathered charges can deliver into the air of the world:

I
Mystery into mystery is this place.
No hiding from the pressing hands
of existence.
But now — dance, dance and sing a song
without a hint of fear.
Dance, dance, and feel with full heart and hear:
Marriage, forage, borage, dew,
laughter after never blue!
Do you know your music changes everything?
 — the way we fly, rest, watch-

It changes all.
Skip and skip the rhythm of
your life's celebration.
Skip, skip and dance the motion
of lifetimes woven
here a tintinnabulation
tapestry of leaf, heart, bone, wind,
word and blessed wood.
Go in peace of whole being…
now and forever.

II

O stone crevasse, angular and cold
and shadowed, moving with heavy time,
stretching, curling, twisting,
we trust you,
for you do not lie
nor harm our nests
nor often speak loudly.
We live in that interface of stone and air,
shivering with the tension exchange of heat and light,
and aware our caustic waste erodes you.
But thank you for the
sand, silt, clay and dust
you give us for our sustenance,
for they enliven leaf and worm,
cricket and spider.
Thank you dear, deep stone
For your peace sedimented generosity.

Big words, small birds—

a cosmic lattice-work it stirs.

Befriend your smallest beasts

and forms on planet Earth.

You hardly know the growth

this love confers.

Mistletoe Deva
(Viscum album)
12/24/14

Ring of water
Ring of stone
Ring of air
   A soul alone.

Hand of water
Hand of stone
Hand of mist
   An embryo.

Tongue of green
Tooth of blue
Lips of bark
   We think of you.

small leaf in the high autumn air
berries feed and birth a feather there

the human heart has grown so vast
but will it know how its love's to last?

Leaf of water
Leaf of air
Leaf of muscle
  Is spreading fair.

Heart of salt
Heart of heat
Heart of sunlight
  Beating deep.

Listen water
Listen stone
Listen soul
  To the speaking bone:

  No time is ever here to tell
  of what your will must do to well
  this world of water, salt and stone-
  to well *this* world,
    this world alone.

Box Turtle Deva
(Terrapene carolina carolina)
12/24/14

What mean you by this stance so bold?
We come armoured only with bone and gold.
No offense do we make nor hold-
all brethren crawling on this planet old.

We merge with berry, worm and fungus.
Spirits freely fly intense among us.
Stars and rain, sun shadow's stain
upon our backs reminds us of days
    when roaming was not a danger,
when long, paved death did not split asunder
our ancient paths of movement,
    our reptilian feet of silent thunder.

The lowly and quiet is also great, you see,
for it's the muted and small that bring forth tree
   and me and thee.

Stance of boldness can be let go;
please sit in quiet and let heart grow.
Think upon your box turtle kin
and all that we are, which includes your
   star-lit souls, pulsing blood and tender skin.

Maiden Hair Fern Deva
(Adiantum aethiopicum)
12/26/14

In so great a posture
we present in the loamy soil,
existence entirely dependent
on the vast mesh of different
frequencies, of energies, that you
see as mineral and plant,
mushroom, water and air.
Only warmth and light are heaven's
difference among these.

Will you presence yourselves
in the fabric of frequencies and energies
that dance and flash ceaselessly
through and around your bodies?
An invitation is always
extended for your consciousness
to be itself with us,
to extend in full dependence

on everything else in all
directions and in all
time through Earth home
and sister planets and all beyond,
beneath one in love,
with all the other ongoing.

Here is love:
that which binds and holds
and links and trusts and sees
no borders, nor any reason
not to be wholly
and fully flowing and invested
in the other.
Love is the thought,
the energy and the feeling
that is the tapestry of stars,
that is the shimmering cloth
into which everything
is woven.

We are that.
We are love.

Wild Boar Deva
(Sus Scrofa)
7/15/15

I, this deva, will share:

Romp though you will on this earthly plane,
so bear in mind that we exist
above not vertically, as you think,
but in all-surround – in etheric glow.

As such, we pull forth much
to bring our charges into being,
whose role is balance and repair,
full use and rigor.
We bring forth love in unfamiliar form

to do this work,
but also to teach that love
may not be lovely form nor moving sound,
nor pleasant smell,
but the stuff of healing and fullness.

So do not take our physical
presence as a measure of
our merit, for in our size and motion,
our grand being, we do a service

as do all devic forms on Earth.
We come as manifested love,
grunt and squeal, loving life
in our function, asking
respect, asking protection
if you, too, are in a mind of blossom
and appreciation born.

Black Oak Deva
(Quercus velutina)
7/8/15

You do not see us when you look upon us.
Forms' fresh hardness and color distract your eye.
We are a moving flow of light and fluids
attracting and sending energies of equilibrium,
healing, information from different realms.
We are multi-dimensional beings telegraphing,
    embracing, feeding, praying in our
        vertical and rooted stance:
   the perfect monks, the utmost mendicants
   of soil and water,
   miners of mineral and stone.

We shine all through the night.
We move with air;
we aim to lift and purify and protect
and enrich and bless the soils,
     and revive our souls
     and recover the songs
     that collect and converge
     the strands of energy
     that make of Earth a whole.

We dance in this vital effort.
Our leaves tremble in celebration!

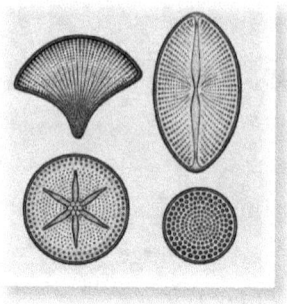

Diatom Deva
7/22/15

Life and water are the same to us-
moving mix of sun and moon,
of galactic mud
which is to say of cosmic breath
and matter serious.

In this celestial brew here on Earth
(you call by pond, lake, bay and sea)
my forms take shape in tiny diaphanous births,
which, to us, are worlds themselves
spinning free, celebrating
fluids touched by lobster antennae
and urchin spines,
roiling octopus and beaming blennies.

Touch this place and our trillion crystal
orbs with your human hearts to renew
yourselves in your worried and separate selves-
illusion, though, that that mind-state is.

Feel us with your mental tendrils,
sing our song of moving, shining facets,
and think upon the oceaning and foresting
made of our billion-year-lives
gently lying atop soft laminations
for your hands to sift through-

those new fingers made of love
recognizing the other, recognizing themselves.

The New Zealand Longfin Eel

(Anguilla dieffenbachi)

9/6/15

O shadowed history of this little noticed world,
we conjure spirit-thought and knit a weave so cleanly
dear and delicate that to a night-jar
we would be seen only in gravity's dim gaze.

Not always blinded by worldly ways
of grasp and take and hold and hate,
human-folk wisely took for granted their
umbilicus to this planet of streaming
steaming, shimmering, briskly, bristly,
slimy life-loving form.

Plowing seas with ships ensued,
and furrowing the soft medium of soil,
breaking one and the other.
Then, in such foolish blindness-
a violence of self upon self
we could barely fathom;
though death, we know, this stage
of planet circumstances embraced.

Shrouded, you all walk-limp, stumble,
crawl, pleading for the redemption you hope
for and therefore does not come.
The stars do not lie - for their telling
of history reveals their origins as human-like
with aspirations of clearest gem,
unimpeded by the thought of love's limitations.

Who are you, dear bi-pedal, dry-skinned,
heavy-boned, skeins of sea water?
You are eel and bear, star and rain,
comet and mud, breath and dream,
light and thus.
Wake up to this and we
wake up Together.

Iridescent Sweat Bee Deva
(Agapostemon virescens)
9/26/15

Come into this tiny opening,
which is my home.
Just a few honey-combed cells
hold our future:
droplets of amber sweet,
eggs and pollen.

A ray of sun visits the chamber
once a day
for a moment or two.
We glisten in our green,
antennae palping.
Very electric, so alive,
even in our stillness.

Who are you in your electric selves?
We must do as we Buddha do:
essential path.
You, who are tethered to nothing
except the stars
and glowing galactic clouds,
what must you do?
...Are *moved* to do? Who are you
in your infinite breathtaking selves?

Eastern Red Cedar Deva
(Juniperus virginiana)
12/25/15

You will leave your bodies, of course,
and eventually. 'Til then, the lessons now
come hard and fast.
You are ready for them.

Our wood, fragrant and healing –
so, too, your hearts, with their
scent of rose, myrrh and apple blossom;
it remains from the first garden.

Open, then, your celestial selves:
no strangers to darkness or light –
both serving the miniscule bundling
grown wide inside of time.

We, each tree, connected by air,
by root, by soil, by bird, by pollen
and by threads unseen.
In error do you see yourselves discreet.

Linked by thought voice, children, feelings
and knowledge born of wonder,
you are shimmering strands –
each person, a blooming nexus.

These solid-looking things – body, tree,
planet, galaxy – so paltry compared to
their unseen energetic selves, which
speak their hearts across a reach of lightyears.

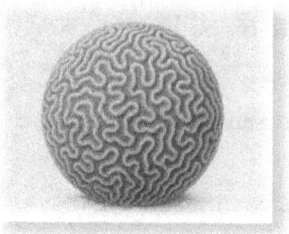

Deva of Grooved Brain Coral
(Diploria labyrinthiformis)
5/16/16

Hum kaa
Haa na'a
Beetoo koojataa

In time and space, the forces flow.
In space and distance, the bent light glows.

In form and stance, the beings we make.
In length and breadth, the forms we wake.

Nee loo faakaa
Beetoo jamaakaa

Our hearts in sync with the cosmos do beat.
Our yearning to create and enliven repeats.

Faa shee balaa
Noo mak atee banaa

So when you see a form before your eyes,
so then the countless energies converge as realized.

Haa kaa ba tee
Koo too hoomee
Balaa na ket
Foo shee ra'abet!

Rocky Mountain Goat Deva
(Oreamnus americanus)
2/2/17

We are sure feet on the hard and stony ledges –

energies pulled together into form and mind

of mountain goat, perfection for high altitude

dimensions, which speak to one another:

    mountain to goat,

    goat to mountain:

    a net of energies

for the perfection high-order wavelengths

to inhabit remoteness and cold

on this full-mesh world.

Where will you go, dear human being?

Look to your minds' orientation and focus,

from whence your frequencies are derived

and to those waves that speak to

(and to whom yours speak):

the whole of the planet,

the sister worlds, beings of energy:

    moons, sun,

    fox, cat,

    known and unknown.

Your freedom is your being's essence.

Grow into unknown places on behalf

of the magisterial mind,

which is the all of everything,

the all of you, the heart of us,

the basis of our sure footing on these

grandly sloped, cool and lonely heights.

Dwarf Palmetto Deva
(Sabal minor)
2/15/17

Skies become ashen, waters brown-green,

sands become barren, roots stiff and mean.

Liken our lives to temporal gravestones,

fanned out across the muck.

You see what you want to –

never seeing us truly: Puck

dancing swiftly in unfurling grace

and waving toward sunlight,

    its energetic face

a sensorial reminder of one energy

beneath, beyond and through.

Skies become golden, waters velvet clear.

Sands become gardens and roots volunteer.

See our lives as they really are:

unfolding receptors of a vast distant light,

holding frequencies from dimensions

where there is never night.

African Bush Elephant Deva
(Loxodonta africana)
4/13/17

Whose ribs are these?

Long-tail breathed inside of them.

And these tusks with acacia stains?

Didn't One-eye use them?

Yes.

I recognize Small Ears skull.

She stands beside me now.

Her low rumble I hear

in my chest and feet…the caress of her trunk.

They have gone from our eyes.

But are here.

We are glad that meerkats

play among their bones.

We taste our family

in the grass and leaves—

not forgetting the footprints

of countless elders who

crossed this savannah before us.

My trunk lifts this great single tusk

in the night air and holds it

high against the shining moon.

We trumpet and weep in exultation.

Bonobo Deva
(Pan paniscus)
11/14/17

We know we come from forest soil

Our nimble fingers grasp its warm

clods and we lift them to our nostrils,

tasting their moldy, darkened fragments.

We savor their history of mingled bodies,

leaves, wood pollen and petals.

Our bodies are animated delight,

moving in moments of time determined

by filtered sunlight's slant and season,

fragrances of fruit and proximal bodies.

We live wholly in our nature

of animated delight.

Which is to say, we live to show

this world a way to live.

Fair humankind-you see us with

lenses and instruments, but you

do not know us, though a handful

intuit our example, our extension

of Earth's ringing affection.

Please yourselves to pause and taste

soils and breathe in their fragrances

of lives passed, each soil

brimming intensity and fulfillment.

Can you bring yourselves to feel

the holy soil beneath your buildings,

around your homes, in your gardens,

graveyards and venerated spaces?

You thus begin from one place

to absorb the meaning of your lives—

lives on this intricately emerald world:

to live in delight, and to nurture a soil

of affection for your extended consciousness—

reaching faint star systems, and feeling

the smallest-pulsed atomic fabric.

Red Kangaroo Deva
(Osphranter rufus)
3/15/18

Of course your science about life functions

is correct, but how small a part of the story it tells!

RNA, DNA, proteins, enzymes—

these are names you apply to what we know as

very specific energy configurations of what

you call elements, but which we call

frequency particles, or light shades more commonly.

How do we work? Templates from the

eons stored in moving etheric landscapes

are drawn upon, and we assemble

the requisite energy configurations and

light shades in a specific place and time.

We then move in what you might call

a virtual dance to draw energy of a

very specific type to bear upon the assemblage,

which creates the organism.

Slightly different assemblages occur in

and among places, due to the changes

in planetry surface conditions.

The variations are indeed selected, but the surface

conditions change according to elemental

commands and cosmic guidance—with Gaia's input.

What means all this?

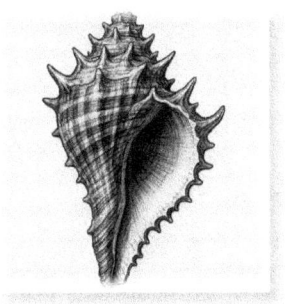

Deva of the Crown Conch
(Melongena corona)
9/16/18

Slow spirals devised

from sacred geometry—

coalesced mineral,

the sand's bones flow

and stretch to reveal our form.

Ancient, rippling, we kiss

the sea floor—our feet are

lips upon the world.

Why are we here enduring

Earth's duration?

Covered by water and shell,

it is time we inform:

We devise a presence

to keep life going.

Given the sureness of catastrophe,

moving slowly in space and time

at the ambient temperature,

works well.

Conchs reserve and preserve,

thus remain and balance,

wed and yoke.

Modulated, elegant, semi-lucent muscles

are intimately stitched

to the architecture

of the human heart.

Elderberry Deva
(Sambucus canadensis)
11/3/18

Walking this way and finding

the path barren.

Singing the path into being before you,

and then praying the path off the surface

into air.

Dreaming the path into every imagination.

The path is the walk, the song, the prayer,

the dream.

But where is the barrenness,

the being, the air?

Where are your hearts?

Small brown eyes shine from

beneath the swamp log.

Fins maneuver a yellow perch

through lilied waters.

Long-leafs shine against the sharp

winter sky.

There hides your center

in the mink's eyes,

the blue gill's fin, the pine's needles,

in the rings of Saturn,

the storms of Jupiter,

between the glowing arms

of the Milky Way.

The barrenness is crowded

with unseen worlds.

Being is suspended like

a torch before you.

And our lungs are the air—

breath incarnate—

the measure of life and pulse

and streaming intent on the

lifted path of who you are.

Seaside Goldenrod Deva
(Solidago sempervirens)
11/4/18

Say to yourself:

Now I am going to bed.

I am going to let my blood relax.

An empty bladder gets sleepy.

Stomach—still with small remains

of apple and ginger—

can become soft and pink

and loosen its grip

on surrounding mesentery.

Now you can leave your body

between the sheets and under warm blankets.

If you choose to help before closing your eyes,

a vastness of purpose opens up.

Your toes wiggle a little

while your hair becomes spun gold.

Pyramids rise and crumble.

The Ganges changes direction.

And souls on other worlds are not unfamiliar.

All the while, you help

something to get done.

It's a work of lifetimes, but—

being an essential thread in the tapestry—

you are elated to meet

with a thousand monks

from ten religions, and to

dance with them dressed

in their graceful robes of saffron

deep blue, purple, black, white and rose.

And their song: full-throated, joyful.

Their song, which you sing

during the dance in your own

lifting voice of oak green—

the song, which is in some lost

and exquisite language.

That song—it builds worlds,

sets stars spinning, breathes dimensions,

and creates an embrace

that sustains every atom

in every universe in

the entirety of being.

Your toes wiggle a little

while your body slumbers.

Galapagos Giant Tortoise Deva
(Chelonoidis niger)
2/6/19

The fine shape of our fused ribs

forming our shell, our abode.

When will you acknowledge your

shells as the home of memories,

experiences encapsulated and retained

so that knowing vastness can

track and ripple its expansion?

Are you here simply to suffer and struggle?

Laughter and love in these dimensions, too—

reflection swimming and the hatching egg:

a tiny reptile head peering out into world fresh.

No, there is joy and warmth here, a sun brilliant,

sweeping clouds, sand in your hair

beneath running feet.

We stop and eat a cactus pad,

raise our heads and look about,

drink from the small stream that

is not dry at the moment.

Our experience counts as no less vital.

Is it any wonder, then, that

the world rests on our back

of fused ribs forming a universe?

Blue Bird Deva
(Sialia sialis)
2/21/19

Swamps and leafy hills,

streams and rushing rills,

these on other worlds, in distant systems,

your hearts can travel to at will.

But few do,

captured by your day-to-day

definitions, identities and habits.

My angelic form, so to speak,

works on those far worlds, too:

blue birds take form.

Witnessed and loved by

myriad conscious souls,

fed and housed by sentiments

of celebration not unlike your own.

We'd have you hear this most intently:

these feelings, intentions, purposes and pledges—

they link you all so that the work

of one becomes a light to the

orchestra of efforts.

Big words, small birds—

a cosmic lattice-work it stirs.

Befriend your smallest beasts

and forms on planet Earth.

You hardly know the growth

this love confers.

Spartina Deva
(Sporobolus alterniflorus)
2/25/19

For we have not been beseeched for millennia.

Therefore, we bow to the beseechers.

We cannot work without manifestation

of sun, water, wind, salt, silt, worm and snail.

Our forces are evoked by the presence

of their blossoming into physicality.

Low frequency is our mentality.

That said, we dance and are merry

in the bringing forth of long, green spears,

glowing at the edge of sea and land,

a richness and a securing of extensions

into the water of production,

of living mass richness,

of root and stem.

Detritus is our friend.

So when you see, feel, sense us,

we are builders of stability:

models for you, beings of human,

to live and thrive within the confines

of what have you rather than

with you have, with you take.

Can you build extensions into the sea with us?

Use your eyes to see with us?

Will you wake to your wide

brilliant, breathing world?

Will your minds and hearts step into

the place of power, wisdom and love

directed by the unfurling all-things spiral?

Spartina vertebrae for the planet spinal!

Yellow Root Deva
(Hydrastis canadensis)
3/17/19

A child, a child, a child—

dancing, laughing, playing, seeing.

The leaf afloat, afloat, afloat—

murmuring, sunning sugaring.

The crown, a town, around—

silver mesh, silver cords, golden rings.

Now smile, now vile, now guile —

in the maze of ignorance and bile.

You sing, you rise, you shake

away the hate, the fake, the bait.

So true, now blue, go through

the gates of hands held wide:

they pray, they lay, they say,

"You energy packets of love—it's day!"

The Deva of Goldenseal
(Hydrastis canadensis)
3/22/19

Interesting that the flat thinking
of turtles and river rocks should come
to bear on your parties and plans.

We know that time-travelers are wise
to your ways, which are highly experimental,
depending, as they do on choiceful experience.

Never come and go without the seriousness
of intention, which is ultimately concerned
with the One's yearning for understanding.

Of what? Itself in totality.
Itself in expansion, in possibility, in expression;
the meaning of vastness, or not.

Come here close and listen:
the crickets song at night is audible
simply because it exists.
My leaves and stems are solid love.

Don't go yet – one last thing before
we get back to forming vascular cells and chloroplasts:
You are thought made solid,
and solid is your thought.

Deva of the Barred Owl
(Strix varia)
4/19/19

Approach the noosphere and living
    dreamscape of your world gently.
It's bristling with light forms, like us,
    streaming and running energies to form.

Each feather, bill, eye, bone of wing
    and scale of toe brought forth
    in its time to fulfill the brimming of
    the ever-shifting existence called nature.

You, too, are fully in this place of
    rivered light and vibrancy directed by the hand
    of human-intention-to-form that
    you call designing god or angel.

And while we each follow our long directive,
    all the streams of frequenced force intermingle
    and play through one another thereby
    teaching everything what to do together.

For everything exists because of us,
      because of oneness building to know itself,
      dying to know itself, swimming, flying,
      rooting and crying to know itself.

There is an image to help you see:
      it's of the tree alit by itself on the tundra,
      in the swirling snow at night.

It is a point of warmth and self-contained calm.
      That is me, the owl-force, and you,
      the breathing human being — a leaf on that tree of light —
      moving in the ethereal wind.

Quartz Deva
4/29/19

While planets and sun-systems slumber,

We grow, align, place and bind

with the tightness of whole sums: love,

which, if lacking, would mean no place

for the incarnate to find and inhabit.

But in fact, we are so fluid that our lacey

arms are here in this galaxy,

and in all others, too—

where heat and configured energies are present.

So we come and sing the minute bundles

together, and, together again in

lattices of white, rose, grey and blue.

When you sit down to think and grow,

your being changes to consider the stones

at your feet.

Some are quartz, built by spirit lights

you usually cannot see,

but are there nonetheless, tending also the minerals in your bones.

And when you stand to re-engage

with the must-dos and must-haves,

these angels continue their work,

mindful of your road,

respectful of your wishes,

forever rustling and singing beneath

your feet in the molecular

heart of the Earth, like microscopic

tolling of infinite bells.

Blue Parrot Fish Deva
(Scurus coeruleus)
5/12/19

We came here from other worlds,

and as nearly the same.

Do dance and water match this place?

We had to ask in earnest.

For the great hand, with fingers of mind,

wishes that we ebb and flow with

chromosomal currents that are amenable—

with a welcoming weather,

mineral, water and light matrix.

How to share the way we build?

First, it is never alone.

A mixing stew of energies,

millions of spirit-patterned waves

intersect and gently direct the

magnified outcome: the manifest fish.

The robes of Rama Krishna—

their folds envelope us.

The folds of ballet corals:

they welcome us, though we permeate

the cosmic dancehalls, always

looking for the place to play

our orchestral composition.

Ultimately, everything we are is

a rich and joyful music.

You are encouraged to listen.

Blackbuck Antelope Deva
(Antilope cervicapra)
6/14/19

Everything is at once.

A plain in Nepal moves with

the veld of another world.

The winds carry pollen across

valleys that lie in the

folds between arm and chest.

But still, we blackbuck are discreet

here in the green Himalayan plain,

walking with wet nostrils, ears erect,

digesting, watching and wombing young.

Though both and all and the discreet

are together simultaneously,

they are danced at different levels—

at different tempos—

but in the same loving sphere of energies.

These moments of our tails

in the warm breeze,

and our majestic horns giving us direction

and connection to the wider world.

Oh sacred hooves and godly rain!

The human "hand" reaches into

blackbuck heart, spine and tongue.

The tingling human skin dons blackbuck fur,

blackbuck color, movement and essence.

When done, we are understood.

You glimpse the soul of grass,

of the banyan tree, of another world's

blue forests.

Rhododendron Deva
(Rhododendron sp.)
6/12/19

Once, here, the timbrels sounded,

the movement sang.

Once, here, the mushrooms hummed,

the moss had voice,

the moon percussed—

percussed a cushion for rivers,

for creeks, for the seeping bog;

had feet and sent forth its eyes

as frogs into the dripping bush.

Once, here, the smallest path,

the widest sky,

the clearest star.

Once, here, the softest soil,

the magic rings inside of trees,

the lightning flare.

"There is no death," the changes sing,

the changes chant,

the shifting puffs.

What is moss? we ask wide-eyed.

Truly it is a weaving of the mud, of the mud,

the weaving of the holy mud and seep.

Once there was a person-child,

a person-child,

a child of path and stream.

She moved behind the deer so soft

and dreamed of being them.

Once there was a person-child,

who laughed with the bowing fern.

We know you are that person-child,

and wait for your undress:

to toss away the clothes

of greed and me and best…

to finally wear your skin

of give and thee and blest.

Broad-clawed Hermit Crab Deva
(Pagurus pollicaris)
7/8/19

How beyond accident it is that a star

is here to power this living world.

We know and experience the rich pattern

of this place—to us a grace unfurled.

No need to wish for better station and effect,

we are it: small trundling perfection—

workingness in the shallows, in our shells,

in a stream of presence over time,

in a solid, swirling murkiness.

Can you grasp that we would do better

if you noticed us with love? With help?

If you knew we are of the fabric, the great

blanket, would lift—a vast quickening dealt!

O that you cherished us as we cherish you.

For that pattern of lovingness is all things,

is the pulsing weave itself, is ever

dense with particulars. And ever light as it sings.

Hippopotamus Deva
(Hippopotamus amphibius)
8/28/19

When descending to create the hippo body,

everything is looked at—the whole situation—

including landscape history,

fabric of other life forms

meshed with weather, geology, climate,

solar position, planetary spacing,

Jupiter's moons, and everything else pertinent.

We have some flexibility, but the circumstances

must be pretty good for the incarnative gathering

and energetic wave patterning

to commence for every hippo brought into manifestation.

Extinction occurs when the place

and conditions are no longer there

to invite us to begin hippopotamus

form and flesh.

Space and events are left vacant.

Other forms—plant and animal and microbes—

are hindered, conditions being less perfect.

Cascade of weakening environmental invitations comes about.

Resiliency of the whole living fabric:

less and less sure for this form.

Hippo devas pull away;

we offer our energies elsewhere.

The sheer fact of diminished locale

brings trepidation to the devic community,

and robust incarnative activity slows.

We have seen planets die.

But also recover as the conscious

inhabitants embrace their place

in the tapestry, and treat it with the

love that they once reserved

only for themselves.

The expansion of the conscious heart

brings health to the physical dimension,

as it does to all other dimensions and frequencies.

As we scan for hippopotamus'

incarnative opportunities,

we now find fewer and fewer.

You have much to learn in a short time.

We wish you well.

Note: May these words not be laid aside due to disbelief and arrogance.
We thank you for seeking them.

Green Darner Deva
(Anax junius)
9/9/19

When sweat and time become

the lament of the bodies,

our rattling presence soothes

the heart in ways unknown.

When flashing lights and jarring images

loosen your teeth, we catch the

biting flies with a deftness unfathomable.

Where do we go at night, which our

large, rounded eyes can't see us through?

Crouched deep in hidden bush and vine are we,

watching the dreams of trees.

Here with you—our bodies celebrating air—

can you think of us other than as

crispy debris on your auto grills and glass?

Our numbers diminish in proportion

to your weakening attentions.

Such a long history on this planet

captured in our form and function.

Can you look at us anew—as kin

that share your atmosphere?

As energies deserving of your devotion?

Siberian Tiger Deva

(Panthera tigris tigris)

9/27/19

For some of us leaving this world,

we look back at the blue-green planet

and see a gem suspended,

an energy manifest,

brilliant among all the stars and worlds.

A great hope exhales from our body collective,

an immense surge of well-wishing,

a cocoon cast 'round the Earth,

its moon, its rings and swirls.

Nothing moves towards or away

except that which handles love a certain way—

by which we mean that it is

a protected place, a sphere where

events cast unfurling:

Waves of lessons learned, perfection realized,

mistakes made and curved and recurved

into understandings for the

incomprehensible heart-and-mind

that spans eternities,

and brings light to the undefined.

Bald Cypress Deva
(Taxodium distichum)
10/1/19

A poem for humanity:

There came upon this world

a force of power and love.

It rested among the trees and vines,

and distilled a thought of wood—

so soft and pliable,

a tender wealth of good and balance,

which, a living whisper,

came to swamp and marsh

where water is reliable.

Yes, to water it was drawn—

to ooze and damp and moist retreat.

But laughter, too, it sought

to keep its cream wood warm.

Ages passed, its leaves turned brown

and dropped to a darkening soil.

Its bark and branches a home become.

Its knees a way to breathe far down.

It observed and felt and changed its home:

it harbored forms of grace.

The air it filtered and left refreshed,

the soild was cleansed and water-combed.

How often do you see these things,

dear body-clad humans of this time and place?

We unfurl our magic every day

and ring with the celebration it brings.

To stillness in fen, in quiet den

you went to feel our presence.

In somber state, tall and true,

in silence you honored we

that bring you cypress,

that bring you wood and water.

You cleansed yourself before we met

so that you could be a mother,

so that you could be a father,

and now, through leaf and bark,

through sap and catkin hanging,

you grow up into the stars so that

you can become a brother.

Red-bellied Woodpecker
(Maleanerpes carolinus)
11/19/19

An encompassing vision expands out from

the tiny space where a woodpecker will be;

a misty vision of the bird-to-come is

seen climbing a trunk or flying free.

What of the Earth remains to

allow that form to fill

with matter is our concern.

Will human-kind care enough to

let ribosome, mitochondria, cell, tissue,

exquisite eye and beak come to form?

Sing now, child, a song of love

for Earth, water, fire and sky.

Sing, now, children, a song of care

for all that wish to come and share.

The dripping sunlight,

the shining water,

the fluid soil,

the lava's roil:

On this world of carbon-gem,

on this this world of feathered wing,

on this planet of meshed and

breathing woodpecker, walrus,

rift valley and fluted stone.

Deva of Horsenettle
(Solanum carolinense)
12/2/19

A ring of bright thought.
    She wandered near the spring where
    surfaced-ruffled water, silently lifting,
    showed where it emerged from the sand,
    just below the tree and branch reflections.

A slight twist of the wing outstretched in flight.

    Afraid of that quietly moving sand
    where the water emerged in slow boiling motion,
    where the water met openness after
    long confinement underground.

They glinted, those feathers, like quick sparks.

    But she wanted to touch that cool birthing
    spring water, so clear and alive, and feel
    the darkness, too, and fathom the veins that
    ran beneath roots, fields and mountains.

Whose eyes see what? Your eyes are a flash to a wheeling crow.

> So carefully at first, finding her breath
> coming harder, quicker, she put her open hand,
> fingers wide, at the top of the sand, which moved
> like a white blanket with baby's toes wiggling beneath.

You create my wings. I fashion your legs.

> She felt the rippling water touch her fingers
> and, closing her eyes, felt her arm deep into
> the spring, slowly, afraid, as far as she could
> reach-the coolness rushing up past her wrist and arm.

We see a landscape together,with its electric netting no longer invisible.

> What endless darkness! – the urge to quickly withdraw
> her arm from the Earth's mystery of roots and stone,
> crevasse and pathways never seen, hewn
> silently over time's long stretches: what stories!

Your eye is my wing, my throat, my tail.

> With eyes closed tightly, images of a living
> thing as big as a world holding her hand,
> knowing her courage, smiling with her head bowed
> in startled gratitude for a large and starry heart.

We both see her tears as she slowly pulls her
arm from the depths of the spring, dripping
with the cool and clear that is feeling daylight
for the first time in centuries.

Bison Deva
(Bison bison bison)
12/10/19

We stand in the sheets of rain

    ragged and dripping

    hearing thunder,

    slight shudder at

    each lightning bolt.

Feeling everything we must:

    presence of calf,

    where the movement occurs,

    shifting rain and wind,

    all the herd.

Drying out, the spirit keeps us

    standing for life,

    tasting the grass,

knowing this place

for a stream of centuries.

The mountains of skulls

bereft of brains,

without eyes,

no steam from wet nostrils

on cold mornings.

Then, almost too late, your love awakens:

a little in your teenagers,

in your children,

in your regretful old ones—

but enough to know that we

can still come to this world,

that we can pull the lightning

of grass and clover together

again into breathing bison bodies,

which are all Buddhas—

nothing but spirit—affection

roaming the wide places.

Scarlet Oak Deva

(Quercus coccinea)
12/22/19

Are we just one final thing?—

said the standing thick-wood tree

with leaves expanded to the sun.

We are, in fact, the acorn and its

minuscule promise, the seedling,

the sapling, the tree come of age

with its roots in communion.

And all the while the intelligent energies

are flowing into and out of oak tissues,

visible to you as acorn, seedling and tree.

Visible to us as webs of pulsing energy

from the immensity of the whole, to the

can't-catch-me moving molecules.

We come forth, we come forth;

we gently extend from the universal

to the particular, from a vastness,

to a planet, a place, a field or forest.

The joy, the splendor, is that

you know this; you feel us—

you celebrate our work: the

germination, the growth, the flowering.

Where is the separation?

Nowhere, really.

Our commune is not only with

fungi and neighbor hickory,

but with you, heart and soul!

Eucalyptus Deva
(Eucalyptus regnans)
1/19/20

Mornings come, and so, too, the versatile

presences of community beings

all dressed in their physical finery

in this binary place

of light and dark, death and life,

photon captured or photon streaming.

We burn so readily—

sap as elixir of flame.

But we made it there

in our leaves,

which can't be to blame because

we can feed only so many insects

and koalas before succumbing.

This race of life against death

is simply an illusion;

we exist regardless, in or out of burning

or slow death and then decay.

There is an energetic heart or core

to all of This—call it what you will.

And that This has its movements and

will and reasons, which—through your tears,

suffering, burning loves, pleasures,

sacrifices—comes to know itself.

And, through that knowing,

is a thing beyond these words

to capture or explain…

is a thing perhaps more loving,

perhaps beyond anything

my branches or your human mind

can retain.

Orangutan Deva
(Pongo pygmaeus)
2/12/20

Seeing the sky cloud up

and sheets of rain form beneath—

the slow patter of drops on broad leaves

quickening to a steady rush

and then a roar, with lightning

and drumming, both far and near.

We fill this place among massive tree,

aware in our marrow that

we have long been here.

In our dreams—for we have vivid ones—

this world in this sun-well is a place

among billions where beings come

to exist in the midst of rain, leaves, soil

and one another.

You can see with our eyes

if you are not afraid—

just as we can see with yours.

So it is not simply to exist among

the tree trunks, street lamps,

roads and flickering technology.

It is also an expansion,

a flowering into this world.

And that is a tale of learning

among the hard surfaces of your streets,

your walls, your personalities, your fears.

Come out and sit in the trees with us.

Listen to the rain begin on the bromeliads.

Dream our vibrant dreams of

a world, every world,

moving full tilt in a spiral arm of stars.

Then stop and discover prayer

for the first time, and certainly, we hope,

not the last.

Turquoise Deva
(CuAl6(PO4)4(OH)8-4H2O)
3/6/20

In the fine structure of our being,

the configuration of minute pulses

determine our form,

color hardness and function.

Beyond that structure, in the stars,

lies our true presence,

which is a hand of the universe,

or rather, a tiny finger among many

that gives the variety of presence

needed to give full life to existence—

to that which strives in consciousness

to seek and advance the basis

of all and everything:

the resplendent one.

We relish our coexistence with so many

other forms you call mineral and element

because it's precisely the vast spectrum of

associations which make the range of possibilities possible—

which bring to light the infinite different combinations

that result in so many life forms, so many worlds,

multitudes of star systems with distinct personalities.

We are a laughing mineral,

and that is just one of the

reasons you love us.

We would say to follow your highest dream,

for that is what we are here to help you to do.

And how would you describe that dream?

From what we've learned of you,

we'd say it consists of raising yourselves to suns,

being stars in the firmament, then, one by one,

expanding into the infinite in a

burst of loving work accomplished!

Coconut Crab Deva
(Birgus latro)
3/15/20

There is no need to connect with us

if you don't want your perspective opened.

We are a curiosity, it seems,

and our flesh a delicacy.

But we have been fitting into specific

landscapes for millions of years.

Two hands, two claws,

the sweet coconut flesh

and tributes to gardens

of vines, our ladders.

The specific energies responsible

for our creation coalesced when

Earth was far younger.

Given the great spans, we changed

form and here we are as you greet us.

Should equally long spans occur,

we would again change in our survival pattern.

How well we see

a world of patterned sand

and a single stony body

crawling across eons, lively.

Dear humanity, we are here

together in form. You collect your treasures

as we our coconuts.

You can open capsules of knowledge

as we open our boulder-hard fruit.

No two feathers are the same,

we've noticed. Yet their

function is nearly identical

when attached to the bird.

How you struggle, rightly, in your

bodies to learn the lessons of love,

of letting go, of standing back

so that wisdom can finally come

to your mind's door.

Laughter moves the

ferns around us, and

song weaves us together

with every mole, mouse and mushroom.

We are not so different, we two beings.

You move from here to there to secure

your monies, foods and family.

And we plod to secure our fruit, space and mates.

To bodies and space we are confined.

No truer thing than this:

we are all fabrics of exploring

extended by cosmic tendrils

into the unknown for answers.

Lady Bug Deva
(Coccinella septempunctata)
4/7/20

No mistakes, perfection here

as we lay the etheric energy lines

for lady bug presence

in this place, this time, this sphere.

We lay out the perfect tiny

form to be realized from egg to nymph

to magnificent: the rapid and

eager and hungry millions are born.

Now you, dear souls what do

you make of us? Little things to appreciate,

to ignore or fear. See us as part of you—

an extension of your eye, your

heart, your celestial anthology.

Yes.

Bluebird Deva II
(Sialia sialis)
4/12/20

Come now to lands of whimsy and
flickering flames, where cares are where
and lies foretold.
This is your land to play in —
The fields of the Lord,
Rainbows or thunder, peace or war.

That dance is ours to support,
To be in, to lift and make whole.
We forces of life-giving and good
move amidst your wills, your thoughts,
your wishes and intentions,
your final works.

And when we perish at your hand,
we energies find our work in
different lordly fields, perhaps a
million light-years distant,
because we, if needed, are eternal too.

My little female may brood her eggs
all according to that which we've instilled
in the sweet marrow of her tiny bones.
Emerging from *your* marrow…what?

The landscapes of tomorrow
populated with every conceivable turn,
but mostly the sublime –
for it's that to which you most aspire,
you souls of this world,
you souls of loving fire.

Sea Lettuce Deva
(Ulva lactuca)
5/20/20

When over the gunwales you throw us,

you barely register our green inflection.

When you sometimes munch on us,

you might nod in our direction.

What you do not see or feel

in this dense place,

are the streams of hued energy

arching down or springing thus

to make our form.

And that is what we truly are.

When we brush against your legs or belly

in the ocean during your swim—

When we wash ashore alone or in rafts,

you walk upon us or overlook us altogether.

Waking up to our presence,

and to the presence of all

other forms in matter,

is something for you to do:

seeing all of us as part of you.

Leafcutter Ant Deva
(Atta laevigata)
6/21/20

And when you sit by the stream

and catch shadows of your hands

over and under the water,

remember that *that* is not your hand,

nor your shadow, but a memory

of the infinite—

our observation of all time.

No one forced you to be here.

Everything *asks* you to be here.

So you bend your light-self into a body—

uneasily—and live out the shadowed

hand over and under the water.

Even so, that hand, that water, that shadow

are exquisite, perfection beyond reckoning.

And your consciousness sees and knows this

and celebrates with song and prayer and dance.

We come amongst you as tiny creatures,

to be noticed as perfection in the setting

for souls frequenced to this vibration,

to exploration, expansion of the vast light,

another flowing arm in the wandflower

of captured eternity.

Cecropia Moth Deva
(Hyalophora cecropia)
8/5/16

Darkness and light upon the wing tips

moving in shadow and sun.

Heavy overlords of distant passions and place

come to crush our sacred space

of mottled green and quiet stream.

Oh do not look on us as art:

the wing of eye and startling presence.

See instead the eons of living, of flying,

    of row upon row of minute white eggs

    on the undersides of a million leaves.

Where do we go from here,

we favorites of wood sprite and spirit?

Voiceless, we fly through dwindling woods

 over paved forest,

 under flying metallic noise,

 between lighted spires—

 all confusion for us and ours.

 Where is the moon?

Can you learn to move with our quiet

and soft-bodied perfection over this green world?

That is our question, our wings unfurled.

Mahogany Tree Deva
(Swietenia macrophylla)
12/25/17

Thrice has our wind-borne spirit

    come to help.

Thrice have you seen but not accepted.

Our drooping hands are bloodied

    and tired.

Our limbs soaked with kerosene

    and set aflame.

Our bodies ripped to thin plates

and jammed into the homes of kings.

Yet you do not recognize us

when we come, when we come

   seeking your help—

our limbs and bodies and roots

   aflame and crying.

How can you ignore our pleas

shouted into a thousand dreams,

into a million hearts,

into a billion eyes?

You cannot piece us back together

once we are burned or skinned, slice

   and scattered.

Our final words:

treat us with respect.

You do not want to see your lands

turn dry, your eyes turn dry,

your blood turn dark and desiccated,

the collar bones and rib cages

of small animals fallen into

the open cracks of beige clay

that was once the floor of our misty home

filled with honey comb

and echoing bird calls.

Humanity's Deva
(Homo sapiens sapiens)
12/27/17

Once there was a rainbow

that filled the galactic sky.

It's colors were the foundation

of a fluid from God's warm eye.

When the fluid fell and vaporized,

the droplets become worlds,

and souls were born to fill

the void of mystery and its whorls.

Curiosity and compassion

are the means by which they roam,

exploring every cosmic crease

and folding gaseous womb.

Today your spirit's arms are long.

They reach with happy freedom.

Yet stuck in mud and dark embrace

is a part of you, a part that needs light's season.

That great and stretching rainbow

has colors you cannot see.

Its spectrum dances and sheds fresh worlds

like fruit from an ancient tree.

It is not so hard a thing to know

that the rainbow's in each heart—

and beats in rhythm with a cosmic pulse:

your impetus to unfold and grow.

Blue-naped Parrot Deva
(Tanygnathus lucionensis)
7/11/18

When time stops and sight begins,

the peeping frog's legs extend.

To see the forest's light-shaft pillars

and climb them to the source of light,

the blackness of perception's void

is nowhere to be found.

Instead, the cosmic fabric is alive

with thought and light-year handshakes,

infused with layers of intent

seeking to be self-taught

by spinning, cloudy, glowing orbs

that reach to pushing rims.

Yes, intended tendrils of thinking light,

we swift to Earth's kind air

and spin the dusty clouds of mass

(congealed intent and thought, that is)

into parrot, child, and bass

whom teach the dancing tapestry,

via azure threads of learning,

to build a cosmos with a tutored heart

still young and stretched with yearning.

Gerenuk Antelope
(Litocranius walleri)
8/3/19

As we create the slender antelope form,

we feel, see, sense the human around us—

    the lion and us

    the grass and us.

We dance with anticipation to feel

the savannah soil under hooves,

    rain on our backs

    sun on our flanks.

A twisted leaf tells us the story of this place—

its water under root,

    elephants under branch,

    leopard hiding prey.

Our star sits center blazing,

powering life on this world, dousing us with

    the vitality of light,

    the impetus of love,

    the feeding of locale.

This home world makes us.

We create the place though our bodies,

    breathing air,

    eating plants,

    feeding lion, cheetah, roots,

    ourselves in death and defecation.

Can all this be illusion?

Our bodies, the dance,

our form and disintegration? Follow us

    to the flowing course,

    to the meaning force,

    to the silent source.

Every form we create is an

invitation to be

    the twisted leaf,

    the elephants' print,

    the rain's signature of moisture.

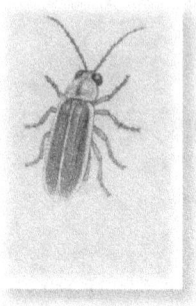

Firefly Deva
(Lampyris noctiluca)
7/8/20

If you could see us—

streaming filaments of flowing energy—

as we work,

your hearts would be filled and settled.

You would not be able to help

having those feelings

because you'd know that you, too,

were enlivened by something the same.

One source of intelligent energy

streaming, splitting into countless

strands and giving rise to all forms—

living or not—

one stream for a plant,

another for a planet.

You, magical humans, can enter

those streams and travel their lengths

to the wings of firefly

or the rings of Jupiter.

Or upstream to the Source,

the infinite start,

and make acquaintance with

the very heart of creation.

White-throated Sparrow

(Zonotrichia albicollis)

7/20/20

Sun, moon, wind, rain—

mountain terrain.

City blocks, hard sidewalks.

Tall buildings, our small nests.

Everything inseparable and we accept.

Hatchlings, mouths open, fledglings—

rich in blood in our tiny hearts—

at night our wings at rest.

Don't you think our natures

are meant to blend with

what we've known for millennia?

Don't you see us as a force

of energy, fractaled into

a million bodies?

Consciously, you rarely do, of course.

But at the core of your sensate beings,

you know all of this:

the countless energies of feathered,

furred, scaled and slick-skinned neighbors.

Some of you have grown up

and can feel, hear and dance

with those signature waves of

thought becoming matter,

possibly becoming this.

Our song helps you to melt

away your personal cages—

just for a moment.

But suppose you flew free

entirely upon the occasion

of having heard our call.

Eastern Meadow Mouse Deva
(Microtus pennsylvanicus)
8/29/20

As we approach your dimension and wave-length,

we sense with utmost exquisite accuracy

the conditions and state of place and time.

If all is right, or nearly so, we work with

all the filaments of energy and direction already here,

and approach the tiny womb of impregnated mouse.

So much time, energy, matter and

effort for a baby mouse!

But that is the hand and desire

of the immeasurable being whose tendrils we are.

It is hard to imagine the demanded perfection:

every whisker, peeping protruding eye,

tip of tail, miniscule rib and flowing capillary

gently placed into being and service to be

a living mouse, both birthing and birthed.

And so with you.

We say you do not yet

know what a cell is.

You do not yet know

its interior of fluid electric

dance and spin.

You barely have touched

with understanding

your own bodies,

much less the intensity

of their connection to

all beings, both here and far distant.

O people, you are mouse and sequoia,

stone and stream, star and light.

You are one another.

Love in this understanding

and become the bearers of joy and bliss,

the singers of the eternal song.

Swamp Rose Mallow Deva
(Hibiscus moscheutos)
9/20/20

Linking up to their soil matrix

is a fascinating thing:

root tips probe and twist

in the darkness,

extending tender filaments.

And so do you, and we all—

gently feeling our way forward

for the moisture of the soil,

for the meaning of the soul.

Pink Muhly Grass Deva
(Muhlenbergia capillaris)
9/10/20

When you walk upon a star

(and you can),

you'll notice first the intense activity,

and you can feel it in your toes.

But upon diving down into its interior

(and you can),

some different observations occur:

the intention of the energies,

their purpose—to release all shades

of radiation for the creative use of

whatever forms and beings are there,

and which dance, sleep, swim and rise

in animated presence on your worlds.

Some of these radiant energies

are unknown to you at present.

But they are all essential to

everything's development,

unfolding and evolution.

These are simple statements.

So back to sun-walking:

eventually you'll notice that you've

become a solar flare,

stretching out far into space,

flashing muscular arms,

fingers flung high,

magnetic gravitational hands sparking

instantaneous magnificent crescendos

of fire and force, glowing turns,

shining expulsions and regathering,

settling on a sunspot.

It feels good.

Who are you, dear human soul in a body?

Nothing less than a charged fractal form

of the origin-creator herself,

shimmering arms spread wide

in creation, observation, celebration

and affection for everything that is—

for all the possibilities lying in her womb,

being born or born anew.

Ruby Deva
(Aluminum oxide)
9/19/20

It is funny and interesting,

when you pick us up, touch us

in a mine-shaft, gem store or as a jewel.

Do you know we immediately read you?

What do we mean?

And why would we do that?

Mineral spirits work to help,

We feel the impulse of your being,

the cerebral and limbic waves,

your heart's reasoning,

your soul's impetus and patterning.

And then our efforts engage

to temper the arrhythmias,

to direct the energies,

to clear your vortices,

to brighten your thinking and empathies.

Ruby sings a specific frequency

designed to advance your growth,

intended to bring you closer to center.

So hold us to your forehead,

to your heart,

to your throat,

to your solar plexus.

Lying your body on the ground

helps the vast expanse of minerals

and gems beneath you to help

in your healing, your evolving,

your resident capacity to love.

We are prayers made manifest.

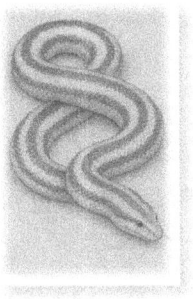

Desert Rosy Boa Deva
(Lichanura trivirgata)
10/3/20

Here we give word to

our devic knowledge.

But first, an interlude:

walking next to

a blackwater tropical river,

you spot the long dorsal fin

of an immense fish

undulating just above

the soft water's surface.

It must be six feet long,

you think, that fish.

But what you don't see

are its gently moving gills

fanning and sifting

the water for oxygen.

Nor its great heart,

beating with the pulse

of a forest rainstorm,

and the arrival of

immense clouds piled

up to the Andes whose

white-tipped spires reach

up to a billion stars.

That great fish,

whose scales are each one a gem,

feels and knows all of this—

the great rain that is to come

in a few moments,

the rush of roiled water afterwards

that tastes like the mountains.

Our interlude ends.

We, the energies of the rosy boa,

are a thousand time more aware

than you, our observing

friend in an Amazon tributary,

so that rosy boa life histories

will unfold as flawlessly as possible

in an arid desert place.

That which fuels our caring

is what you sometimes call love—

    the endlessly streaming heedfulness

    of the universe into the physical world—

    your world of a few dimensions.

We, rosy boa, ask that you

do not wholly lose yourselves in the physical…

in this world of limited dimensions

and lost perceptions.

In understanding your godliness,

you awaken to that same kind of love,

that excited, natural, flowing stream

of caring so much needed

by this injured world.

Please handle us gently.

Western Cattle Egret Deva
(Ardea ibis)
10/16/20

Every once in a while
it's good to go far afield:

Landscapes unfamiliar.
Unknown living forms
invite closer examination
and hatch curiosity.

So in these places —
your feet being careful,
your eyes trying to identify –
you catch a glimpse
of things observing you.

For a moment you identify
deeply with those beings –
the nameless tree moss
and mineraled rock –
and see *yourself* as
the unknown entity.

Fresh you see yourself –
a light moving between
a mesh of perspectives –
and you can never
be the same again.

Laughing Kookaberra Deva
(Dacelo novaeguineae)
10/24/20

Bring your wooden sticks, flutes

and hollow reeds to the fire.

Play a calming rhythmic sound.

Let your head, shoulders and backs

move with the sound

seeping into your marrow.

Long ago, we awaited your arrival,

and we have watched your movement

on the land and through water.

Your eyes, but especially your bones,

could feel song-lines

crisscrossing the mother terrain.

Your feet could follow these lines.

What a disruption when broken brothers,

who'd once known the song-lines of their lands,

arrived hungry to possess.

Minerals and trees shook.

We birds flew away.

The eyes above and embedded

in dark skin wept in dry caves.

All of that to learn

the lessons of remembering

and of keeping the sacred:

the Earth is a great gift

upon which hearts and minds

are to rise up on the stage of orchestration,

expanding into and creating vast spheres

of harmony where learning

and caring go hand in hand.

Bird of Paradise Plant Deva

(Strelitzia reginae)

11/1/20

Only a strong musk smell

does the job of opening your

olfactory organs to the task at hand.

It can be a sweet musk,

but the Earth element is vital.

Sit with hands folded across your lap.

Your breathing: calm and steady.

Now you can be a leaf.

A long leaf near the top of the plant

receiving sunlight and holding it

just long enough to create what you call

chemical energy but is, in fact,

layered frequencies, ballooned vitality.

This is happening throughout

the trillion corridors of

your long, graceful green self.

And in all your systems.

Maximillian Sunflower Deva
(Helianthus maximiliani)
11/17/20

Seeping all through these patterns

of light and force and waves

is the silent presence.

What is that, pray tell?

It is the calling unknown,

fantastically exploring itself.

And we sunflower spirits,

why do we be in this

unfolding through light years?

To hold soil tight against Earth's breast;

to feed bee and skipper;

to brighten, enliven, give air

and die into the roots of future plants.

We help the Explorer, in brief.

As do you.

So breathe with us and hold

your palms out as

we do our created leaves.

Imagine, then, that every star's light

is captured by your hands—as it is.

Any wonder that you are speaking with us?

We are not very different

from the spirit of children,

nor of those just died

and entered into wonder.

Eastern Grey Squirrel Deva
(Sciurus carolinensis)
11/22/20

Imagine how small the ribs of our newborn young,

And perfect eyes unopened as yet.

So as minerals and fats and

amino acids assemble,

the rib lengthens, the eye opens

onto a world of near perfect fit.

This is what we do, you know,

in service to Earth,

on behalf of you, other forms,

and the universal presence.

No, not a task, but

joyfully undertaken

like red corpuscles dropping

oxygen off at the doorstep of

your ardent neurons, retinas,

narrow muscle fibers.

There is a laughter in building squirrels,

which is one reason spring feels good.

Now you can gaze upon your

own body and understand

why a smile appears naturally

on your face—

and why your baby returns that to you

in perfect innocence and grace.

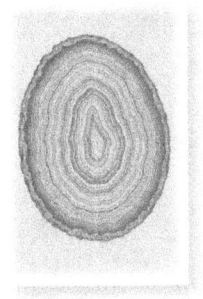

Agate Deva
(Silicon dioxide)
11/30/20

Here is a temporal lobe

and space where you all dance

your steps, sing your song.

This is the place, the space

where your dreams are fulfilled:

so mindfulness is your key to

create dreams that

will carry you and all

to the center of your best.

When shadows appear,

do not jump.

They are yours.

Look at them closely

to find the outlines

of fears and doubts.

Trace them backwards

to see their origins,

and then love that place.

Agate presence here on Earth

is shimmering with

the energies of birth.

Collect yourselves and rise,

not Lazarus-like,

but like a newborn's eyes:

like that single star,

the horizon's prize.

Fly Agaric Mushroom Deva
(Amanita muscaria)
12/20/20

There it is!

The flashpoint when you see

something for the first time

even though seen before.

It is we speaking to you.

Whether moist dark tree bark

or tiny yellow flower,

we are entering your heart's mind.

You pause, awakened by the delight,

and a little stunned by the realization

of your usual stupor,

enforced, as it is,

by the strength of

mistaken identity and the lure

of individuality at all costs.

Walk, then, the path of surprise

so that toad stools stir

you to the depths.

So that the feather on the ground

overwhelms you, for a moment,

with wonder and expands you

into the mystery of flight.

Azara's Agouti Deva
(Dasyprocta azarae)
7/2/20

Wholly what we are is what we are:

occupying a place of motion and activity,

a bodily place on this planet,

given to that clear presence

of gases, waters, plants, shade and warmth

where we are welcomed, healthy, eating and eaten.

On other worlds, the same occurs:

the forms fill out in spaces where

the fit is good, where a role is

called for by the exquisite mix

of other now-physical beings

akin to Earth's plants, microbes,

animals, fungi and what-have-you.

And all everywhere called into being

by the will and desire, if you will,

of the single and only presence

that you might call the holy one,

but who is, to us, simply our

food, sunlight, water, movement, stillness—

the unnamed gathering

of which we, and you, are a part.

Chipping Sparrow Deva
(Spizella passerina)
1/10/21

Only once has this moment existed

in its flourishing masterpiece

of endless colors and movements flowing.

This moment, when

the vast void writes

her name yet again

on the eternal canvas

of what is only now.

Then you know your part

as a rainbow dollop

on the ethereal canvas:

to move with every suffused

extension of yourself,

touching everything else.

Knowing, then, what you are,

you gaze undistracted

at her expanding self, a void so full

of all creation's learning—

expanding dimensionless—

that your breathing stills

and your blood surges

without need for pulse.

Mountain Gorilla Deva
(Gorilla beringei beringei)
1/17/21

There were three boys throwing stones.

Throwing stones they were.

Said one to the others:

Where our stones did land,

let us look for them like brothers.

So, one, two, three, they skipped to find

and looked between the leaves.

They strove and searched but did not

find those stones with any ease.

When they gathered again,

breathing hard, you know,

they laughed a bit and then related

what they had found so low

amidst the grasses, brush and leaves.

One said he found a light and

the others wondered at that.

"By light, I mean the insect lit when touched

--that is what I mean."

They all nodded and sat so still

that they jumped when another spoke.

"I found a queen ant all red and black

surrounded by her children."

the boys sat in wonder

and looked up and out afar.

Then the third spoke up quickly

to relate his find uncommon.

"I found a tiny person crouching against a tree.

I held my hand out in friendship

and the little person approached me.

She said she lived within the wood,

within the tree, and did not

expect to be seen by me.

She then dissolved before my eyes

and became a tiny orb of light.

She parted with these singing words

before she left my sight:

> "The queen ant is my sister,
>
> the lighted insect my child.
>
> This tree will feed upon the stones
>
> you three have thrown, beguiled."

Yes, the boys were changed that day

and grew to be old men.

But they never looked at stones

nor crawling things the same way again.

Northern White Rhinoceros Deva
(Ceratotherium simum cottoni)
1/24/21

Tethered to the planet still

by the breathing and warm muscle

of the last two forms still alive.

We are attenuated and slowing—

and a kind of grieving has begun,

though we grieve more for the wider world

that has brought this about.

That these two forms of grace

and vital function

convey the signal of extinction

means that things have changed.

What becomes of our broadcast

and pattern after the last are gone?

An African steeped in the long love

and feel of the land will sense

the rhino imprint in the air

and savannah for a few generations.

But as we withdraw

(there are no new conceptions to build upon),

the soil-bound memory fades

except for their bones, which,

like short lengths of light

beneath the soil,

illuminate the rooted myths

and ultimately become

the minerals of star-bound gifts.

Queensland Bottle Tree Deva

(Brachychiton rupestris)

2/10/21

Sands and wind, Pharoah's ink.
The long winds that dressed seas and mountains
with dust from these lands
that settled in Pharoah's ink
and made it gritty and durable.

That ink that came long after the
song lines, the lilting phrases sung
to us by you young dark humans
dressed in skins with ink on
        shining faces,
        with bouncing shoulders,
        shaggy hair.

Then you were our friends.
You knew us in song and chants,
in walking feet, and with hands that
touched us reverently knowingly.

We walked the song-lines with you,
and lightly touched your hearts
with our glowing fingertips,
with our images of vast trees
   deeply rooted,
   soundly, firmly
   grounded

in these sands and winds
and reluctant, vanishing waters.
we were in love with you –
  and still are.

Where now are your strong
arms and feet and songs?

Carolina Praying Mantis Deva
(Stagmomantis Carolina)
2/13/21

We have turned our heads

and watched you walk past us

for a river of millennia.

Some of you saw us swaying

on our legs as if

a leaf in the breeze.

Mostly we were not seen,

which was good back then.

Our energies go toward

far fewer mantis forms today—

we have fewer places to stay

and much less to capture as prey.

So we are quite diminished.

Therefore, so are you.

As the world's life becomes more scarce,

you, humankind, have less force

to be comfortable here—

to be happily planet-meshed.

Your illness and despair reflects

your missing reflection:

you have not prayed

with us for a long time.

Great Black-backed Gull Deva
(Larus marinus)
2/14/21

A shared view of the beach

    is always welcome.

Mists and shallows rippling

    with fry and minnows.

Ghost crabs skitter or stalk,

    then pause and disappear.

This place, where a continent submerges

itself and invites whole new life-weaving

into its descending flanks,

is a bidding to plunge in with your curiosity,

    human migratory excitement

    and affection.

It is largely my world, too:

the thousands of forms it sends up

are my sustenance and the regurgitation

for chicks who wait for me in their

downy selves—wings just tiny intentions.

Here's what you must know:

your warmth toward my forms

and their world, extending from

rain forest canopy to Mariana Trench,

makes evident your connection

(dependence on, enmeshment) with them.

You know your link is slipping away

when your conscious appreciation of

    and love for

    the natural world falters.

Breathe fire into your love of me,

and all that upon which I depend.

You learn far greater lessons

    when you do this...

lessons that extend to other

star systems and dimensions

about which you know

    very little at the moment,

but correctly suspect to be

an element of your heart's domain.

Narwhal Deva
(Monodon Monoceros)
2/8/21

Each evening, things happen

in the great descending of surface forms,

and in the mass rising

of the more submerged:

sunlight and then moonlight.

Our lives in this swirling world

of eternal waters' movement,

of clear liquid press against our skins,

has us pausing at the surface.

On nights when the wind has stopped,

when the ice is still,

and spaces open for us to breathe,

we point our single tusks to the sky,

to her moon majesty,

to the Earth-child moon beaming.

In our ceremony, a slow-moving circle and song,

the young in the center,

our rhythm and our music embody narwhal

heart-felt love of one another,

of the ocean's vastness as home,

of the Earth in her mysterious ride

near the edge of a galaxy

whose luminous form is like our circle,

here at the surface of cold water,

near the pole of this sacred spinning world,

and among the sparkling plankton of the Vast.

Ocotillo Deva
(Fouquieria splendens)
3/17/21

Who breathes? And when?

What is water? Warm wind?

Emerge from your ten thousand

year cave and take a look.

Rivers with running water.

Bears catching salmon.

Bones becoming soil

after being chewed on by mice.

Here's the freedom

to perceive with a silver clarity,

to think outside the prefabricated

mesh you were born into.

Long and slender is my desert form.

Covered in flowers and humming birds.

Next time, bring your new eyes to me.

Bring your new mind,

your fresh heart.

Next time, bring your whole self—

the one that's made of silence,

bone and diamond light.

Pill Bug Deva

(Armadillidium vulgare)

3/18/21

Dark and damp

under and cool

we flourish.

Our tiny form

segmented, many-

legged, turning

fibered leaf

to loamy soil

across vast areas

of this generous planet.

Like countless species,

we cannot work

in solitude,

but with microbe

and worm, ant

and water.

We build rich

grounding for

sun-energy forms,

green and huge—

no nothing alone—

collaboration all.

Bristle Cone Pine Deva

(Pinus longaeva)
3/20/21

We dream too:

of extending roots clear to Earth's center,

of needles that last for centuries,

of rain that runs between branches

and pools in trunk-base fissures.

And we are aware of your dreams—

the ones that slip out of your hearts—

those strange dancing muscles

sitting in your orchestral centers.

So we see those ephemeral dreams, yes.

By "we," we mean jack rabbit,

reindeer moss, us, and countless others

attuned to humanity's streaming heart messages,

which, counter to intuition,

are truly different in that they have a distinct sound:

a ringing flute-bell-cavern call

that reminds everything on Earth of

why you are here: to dream for the world,

for this solar spin, for the cosmos with its

roots extending deep to the planet's axis.

That's our dream, too!

Deva of the Marbled Salamander

(Ambystoma opacum)
4/20/21

There was a well, deep and cool,
And the water at its depths was perfectly clear.
The sides of the well, carved rock,
Were clean and straight.

In this well, which was oft forgotten,
Lived a being, a spirit-being,
That moved rarely – only now and then.
It was the sound of wind and birds
Above that prompted her movement:
A shifting and alertness.

This being, this spirit, was none other
Than the dreams of children –
Their collective hopes and yearnings.

Wind and song of birds lifted
This being, lifted her so that she
Raised her blue and green head up
To ponder the lighted opening above.

One day a muscular wind blew and
Jays and red-winged blackbirds sounded loudly.
To the well's lip the spirit being was drawn,
And she peered over the limestone edge –
Her algaed-hair dripping –
At the world.
A world with no impositions,
No systems of belief, of rules and repressions –
Just the world as it is:
Clear as the well's water.

Our spirit-being crawled out fully and
Lay on the grass breathing the wind,
Listening to the wren and wood thrush.
And she kew what she must do.
Rising, standing, she spread her arms
And sang a lilting, buoyant song.

It echoed everywhere,
And became part of the tree sap and fluid
In every plant and creature.
But most important,

It open the heart of every child on Earth,
Allowing each one to see true –
Releasing new and gripping dreams into the world
And onto the feathered backs of
Owl, thrasher, kinglet and cockatoo.

Bluestreak Cleaner Wrasse Deva
(Labroides dimidiatus)
4/25/21

Let us show you what it is like to create a cleaner wrasse.

The gathered energies, directed by us,

are focused with great care on

the tiny wrasse organs of generation.

Once sperm and egg are coalesced

in the nest of water and sand,

we guide all initial molecular activity—

for this is a critical moment.

Certain nucleic acids, as you call them,

(we call them creation catalysts)

are formed, activated in the cellular matrix

and guided to build additional cells—

division and so forth as you know it.

But none of this can happen if

the larger surroundings are not suited

to the expansion of the organisms within it.

All energetic curatorial entities,

dimensional conditions, frequencies

(what you would call temperature,

water purity, mineral ratios, substrate sufficiencies

and mix of surrounding living forms—

the ecological community and context),

must be within certain parameters for

the new cleaner wrasse form to grow

and mesh with the world.

We guide through minute fields

of forces and cellular placement so that

wrasse fin gill, spine, gut, eyse, scale

and heart occupy the correct place

in the solid fish shape,

and perform in the correct manner.

And then the magic of happy wrasse

(for happy and sad they truly can be)

comes forth: large fish cleaned of parasites

and debris—the reef tapestry in health maintained,

the ocean space kept going.

The planet, in its evolution,

continues via the assiduous work

of a multitude of wrasses,

given life by the flowing grace of the unseen

"we" who usher them into existence.

Red Mangrove Deva
(Rizophora mangle)
4/27/21

Like entering the empty conch shell,

you wind your way in running,

breathless, pausing to wonder

at the wall's striations and colors

inside the mollusk's translucent home.

Farther in, your run

getting smaller and smaller

until the corridor coils

twist to a close and

there you are: microscopic.

Catching your breath,

you observe what's near:

the shimmering orange lines

where shell was excreted by

a battalion of glands in unison.

And the quintillion atoms

of calcium, phosphorus and sulfur

linked and vibrating with the

energy of ringing cicadas.

From wonder to deeper wonder

you pass until the final

doors open into what can

only be called love.

What else could sustain all this?

The shell, the water, the organism

and everything else?

It's only your self-concerns

and truncated perspective

that keep you sequestered

from the Everest winds of

what's happening in this

moment of impeccable majesty.

Water Silk Deva
(Spirogyra porticalis)
5/19/21

In terms of your understanding of us,

we are empires yet unexplored.

    When they came to the top

    of the dry ridge and looked over,

    they saw a watered and green valley.

These places—of sentient energy

waves swirling life into existence—

fill a near-infinity of pockets,

discrete and rounded,

in the fluid matrix of presence

you sometimes call the universe.

That view attracted them.

So, stepping carefully,

they descended into the

green and watered valley.

To us, the silent builders,

each form is created for its function

in the exquisitely detailed fabric

of your rounded, discrete living

nexus called planet, called Earth,

Pachamama.

And there, settled as a single entity,

a harmonious community.

But individuality and its freedoms

broke through with its barriers, its predilection

to separate in fear, in anger, in suffering.

We will your valleys and ridges,

watered or not, green and soft,

or hard and gray.

You've journeyed into separation

and found it wanting, waiting.

    Through these words,

    meager though they be,

    we invite your broader consciousness

    to play at creation's doorstep

    with us in the far larger

    green and watered valleys.

Indian Rock Python Deva
(Python molurus)
6/2/21

You each have a desire, a yearning,

to sit quietly on the floor

of a forest in silence.

There, the sounds around you

become the invitation and

entryway to your attention:

the movements of small things

under the leaves and twigs,

insects and birds calling,

leaves shifting in the wind.

Where do you go from here?

Into the tree trunks

to bathe in the streaming sap?

Into the eyes of the

green mantis, praying?

When you're there in solitude,

you find the countless

doorways of connection—

in reality, extensions of you.

Walking through each opening

with your heart and mind,

the welcoming is palpable.

You are greeting yourself---

a far larger you, now us.

And you are here, clear light,

sitting on the forest floor.

Zebra Jumping Spider Deva
(Salticus scenicus)
6/5/21

A torrent of expectations are laid on you,

almost from birth:

look like this, become that,

behave, be-have, be half!

What if you stepped away

and stood among the leaves of grass?

Simply looked at trees—

their quiet, majestic presence?

Or considered the new-born

as a great and natural unfolding?

Eager to see, to embrace, to taste

so that some sense can be made

of the exactly infinite rays of being

that surround, give rise to, and create

that electric body of fascinated

and reaching sentience that is

not only the child,

but the universe herself.

Indigo Bunting Deva
(Passerina cyanea)
6/21/21

Calling, calling out to the wider sphere,

the wider sphere of life –

Are you able to hear?

Tragic is the moving stone

that is the closed human heart–

a heart that has suffered long

and flown towards the caves of protection.

but that's the problem –

those caves lack connection.

There, within the mountain

of broken dreams, of shaded eyes,

of dried up streams,

is the abandoned fountain.

Now you must tunnel

to find one another,

and in doing that, scrape

off you centuries of armor.

Let the mineral walls clean you.

And when you find each other

after all that labor,

you recognize those faces, new:

those faces human, elephant-like,

vulpine, feline, dolphin-shaped,

beaked like a parrot

and also blazing like the brilliant face

of your granular, ever-spilling and radiant sun.

Virginia Mountain Mint Deva
(Pycnanthemum virginianum)
7/4/21

Bumblebee settles on my many flowers,

almost rampaging across their surfaces

finding some nectar, a little pollen.

She feeds herself and her young,

brooding beneath the soil's surface in a

hollowed space: larval young, plump and squirming.

A plant can know all of this, and more—vastly more.

Our spirits' smokey form goes everywhere,

explores everything; we must.

No, it doesn't make sense when you

take out your abacus and try to figure.

That's because we're mind-shaped into matter.

Or is it matter—things that matter—

shaped into thoughts? Walk with us please,

into these places you imagine vague.

It's here where reality is sprouting:

the reality of your cities and anthologies.

And, just as important, the reality

    of a larval bee,

    a nectared flower,

a firefly lighting the night

beneath a fern.

Come and learn.

Peyote Cactus Deva
(Lophophora williamsii)
7/18/21

There are times when a scorpion

rests at night sitting on top

of my form in the desert.

Its quick movements and astonishing

awareness are felt inside

my soft gray folds.

I welcome the scorpion and all

other lives, moving and still,

that visit me.

Some come to feel my energies

or to share theirs: earthbound stars

moving or rooted among the Inca-fitted pebbles.

Rattlesnake and rat, owl and ant,

and a lizard that flicks its dry

tongue near my skin.

This isn't a picture of human imagination,

but my living existence here in the open,

under a sliver of moonlight.

When you consume me,

this entire universe enters your body,

seeps into your cerebral folds,

enlivens your awareness.

A wise human knows what she is seeing,

can make good use of this helping experience.

But most people are dull.

You do not know what to do when

the owl's wing brushes your shoulder,

the mouse paws your toe.

Like me, like we, you should know

to stand up out of your dry skins

and lift into the wind

that will bear you across desert and grassland

over forest and tundra in search of the origin,

the ringing centers of heart and hand.

Olive Tree Deva

(Olea europaea)

8/4/21

Seldom do we get your attention,

though our fruits build your bodies.

Look at our most ancient mothers,

with folded, dark and rough living wood.

Close to Earth, we marry her warm flow

with that of stars, sun and Milky Way.

Long before you were here,

we fed the bird, tortoise and deer.

Long after you are gone,

we will do the same.

Where will you go, you clever,

ravenous humans? Who will you be?

And thinking about what?

Rooted and quiet as we are, we know:

after exploring mahem and breath,

you will fly.

Not to anything here, of course—

unless to serve the young of other worlds.

But to the far wider, truly unbounded

realms of mind, will and intention made into fresh expanse:

expanse like honey's long drips in sunlight,

expanse like sargassum's oceanic spirals over a million years.

And there, kind spirits, finally

you'll melt into your true

mass times the speed of light squared,

which we feel every day under our roots—

feel in our plumb fruits, our bent branches,

and our grey-green leaves dripping dew,

sunlight and prayers.

Ringtailed Lemur Deva
(Lemur catta)
8/12/21

There is a little boy, dark-skinned,

silky black hair, living in your country

called India, city of Mumbai

who is fascinated by us.

The mere mention of "lemur"

makes him jump up.

Eyes wide and bright with engagement,

he shows you pictures of us

that he's drawn.

And you see how delight

flows from his fingers as he describes

our features.

When he explains our tails

needed for balance,

he cannot contain himself,

and his arm reaches out behind

himself, as if to stroke

his tail, ours, in affection.

What do you make of this:

a person so alive to our presence

that he is made healthy

just thinking about us?

Do you consider the bond that

reaches from Madagascar to India?

And the ancient connection between

those two lands where India

tore away from Africa long ago?

This is an element to consider.

And we could mention a million

other children, spread across continents

and islands who have similar bonds

to a wide landscape of forms,

from mosses to falcons,

from zebras to cuttlefish.

There's a part of your heart

that might want to pay attention

to this phenomenon—it's born in the curling,

moving, fibrous links between all life forms,

one to the other: evidence

of a deeply felt promise.

That part of your conscious heart—

let it take notice of these children

and their love of the world's forms.

Perhaps then you will rediscover

the animal or plant that stirred

you at night in your childhood dreams

and asked you to listen closely

as it whispered where it lives,

and also why it dwells there

in your young and open heart.

Eastern Oyster Deva
(Crassostrea virginica)
9/8/21

May the sun warm your bodies,

the air refresh your lungs,

the water cleanse and enliven you!

Sun, air, water are our domain, too.

We feed, cleanse and bring habitat,

like so many other forms on this world—

this world that spins out a spreading,

spiral of energies broadcasting to

this universe its singular experience.

Not two of us are alike, like you.

And we pile one atop the other.

We love our company and encrust to cities.

Speaking very softly, water's currents

bring us food in our stillness,

in our fluid matrix of sun, water and air.

Respect us as essential equals, for we wage no wars.

Our silent hymns stream out through all

ocean's currents and rise, like tides, into salt air.

These, too can feed you–

perhaps better than our silvery,

thin bodies of muscle increasingly rare.

Neuse River Water Dog Deva
(Necturus lewisi)
9/14/21

Through you intent in ancestry

in the millions of souls preceding,

you might appreciate ours, too.

In this river system over

tens of thousands of years (as you call them)

we have existed, have managed

through shifts of land and water

difficult to comprehend if your form is human:

low waters, fluids freezing, too warm,

extreme pollution, then dams, floods, dryness.

Tree shade and coolness of flat stones

protected, but so too our repertoire

of behaviors: determination, eternal calm,

robust omnivory, large eggs embodied

with our cellular wisdom.

While the grand swirl of forms

that water us more constantly

keep us in our blessed niche,

these same forces react and twist

and face in your direction when you think of us.

Think of us often, then, with affection

and appreciation--for the vitality we bring to your rivers.

And for what we are: defined protoplasm spread out

among your waters, many thousands strong,

moving with calm deliberation,

rarely seen, still here, maintaining

balance in the living—a kind of laughter

in your waters, a sound heard by the

shading trees and the cool,

wet stones each morning.

Virginia Oppossum
(Didelphis virginiana)
9/28/21

Taking time to ginger-bond the slack,

we matching colloids sink beneath

the resin dews on tree bark.

Don't you feel the laughing cat's rhythm

in her pounce, in her sleek, whispered bounce?

No, you don't have time

or your ego's at stake.

When the elephant garlic is done,

when its fragrance is melted into your nose,

then, *then,* you lift your arms to a new sun.

Whisked away to places never seen—

to lavender hills and blue machines

that are alive, called forth by intention alone.

No, you barely have an inkling

of the meticulously-layered universe,

of the smackling lips of what's real.

Blown down trees and turtle eggs just hatched—

imagine the things needed to put these

on a beach or across the running stream. Imagine.

And when you finally blink a scent

of ginger buds spreading underground,

it's often too late—your eyes are closing.

Our advice is to know your body's

short life, and to green-walk your way

wide awake to every bee buzz, skunk smell and hug—

to be a soul, awkward, infinite

and dripping wet with gratitude.

Indian Pipe Deva
(Monotropa uniflora)
10/6/21

A young teen walks in the woods

trying to fathom or forget her troubles.

We feel her footsteps on the path

long before she passes us, unnoticed.

There are moments when thoughts bloom

and open bright for us to see

in the forest's damp and shadowed air.

Other thoughts are themselves dark patches.

In the immensity of your creative acts,

we are breathless with admiration.

But so far, this profusion has

been mostly self-serving.

When you begin to turn your powers

toward helping us, as you are,

we can hardly imagine the wideness

of the healing winds you'll bring.

Our troubled teen on the path

will then see us, blooming white,

near the forest floor, and pause

in wonder—the way we see her.

Speckled Caiman Deva
(Caiman crocodilus)
10/16/21

Though mostly water-bound,

we walk the forest trails

with you as our eyes, our senses.

It is not hard to be inside

a person who is clear and open

and quick with its senses, its step, its skin.

A skin she sees as holding in her blood, her bones, her organs—

but not her essence nor her wind-borne thoughts

which travel up the rivers

where he sleeps, where he dreams

of the white snow peaks where the waters are born.

Our body forms crawl out

onto the sun-drenched sand and look around:

the butterfly shore, our mouths slightly agape with teeth.

We know you are near.

We have walked the paths with you

and seen the red parrots,

tasted the fallen sweet figs.

We catch a fish, a turtle, a crab and live.

But you—man, woman, child—

must have your dreams to live:

must go to the peaks in your sleep

and stand up in the deep blue of those places,

those places where rivers begin as cool drops

at the edge of a rough, ancient and decorated stone.

Oyster Mushroom Deva
(Pleurotus ostreatus)
10/30/21

Many years ago, when moons filled the sky,

bright fans of energy came to Earth and sang.

Their songs littered the heat and rock

with a formula of tested and true notes:

sounds made organic and decipherable

by the rock forms, by the dimensions of heat.

And root they did, taking in the young world

in order to grow into tectonic symphonies.

Dazzling—that you find it in fossils,

that you feast upon it with your senses today.

But it is so much present that you

forget your immersion in it.

And that forgetting is hurting both the world and you.

It is the source of your diseases,

your conflicts, your unhappiness and poverty.

Now, with one mom, you find yourselves struggling.

And that writhing and pain is helping you to turn,

to turn your senses towards us, the bath of life

in which you can swim with wider strokes.

Your rejoining the orchestra is wanted and necessary,

for your notes are teeming with the luminous vibrancy

of those first thoughts made audible, then tangible.

The word, the word that you are,

and which serves as the vowel-sounds

that complete the sentient sentence

in this chord-driven phrase of the universal song.

Bluegill Deva
(Lepomis macrochirus)
11/18/21

Building water-bound creatures is not so hard.

Water is alive and so it helps in the making.

There is such an astuteness and intelligence

in all liquidy forms—a level of awareness

missing from breathers of air.

We say this so that you'll appreciate

the different realms that cradle life—

from fiery, molten habitat to the

thinnest of air, and indeed space itself.

But here in water, on Earth,

there is such a closeness,

such a dependence on water's alacrity,

that land forms must carry it

in their arteries and veins,

in their vascular systems,

and you must pump it through bodies

rather than simply let it swirl around

your whole being bringing its gifts through

the efforts of sunlight, wind and current.

For you, religions are often born in deserts.

Because there is such dryness,

water is sacred and understood.

Think, then, how grateful we are

for the wateryness of this world.

Our job of pulling together the

exclaimed punctuation of fish

becomes a continuing joy—

a festival of gill, fin, scale and perfect

layered muscles all aligned just so

into the movement of eye, mouth

and two-chambered heart.

Date Palm Deva
(Phoenix dactylifera)
11/25/21

There is a warmth that only

life can bring to the sands.

Together we build this world

of flowering dreams,

where our purpose and thoughts

create dunes and hidden streams.

You can see us as the breeze

moves our dancing leaves,

and feel us when you stand

near the bending reeds.

Only bashful souls tread

near with open hearts

to gaze quietly at the

trove of fallen flower parts.

The bright green light in

children's chests who approach

guides us a bit – and the

light of their bodies push and coach

us with their yearning to help:

their kindness flows from

the kinship that's felt

before the cerebral surmise.

Perhaps they seek our

sweetness when they come.

But it is we who seek theirs—

it's the building of trees that gets done.

Aye-aye Deva
(Daubentonia madagasgariensis)
12/19/21

Serene masters of the swirled energies

make song, make dance, make form

on this sphere-world of shimmering

      gas, solid, liquid,

        heat, freeze, vapor.

We make our dance, too, in the shadow

of branches at night when

the stars' lighted hands open

      egg, chrysalis, seed,

        warmth, cool, moisture.

There are no boundaries to the notes

we sound through the canopy,

through the soft leaves that

      unfold, extend, twist,

      in light, in dark, in stillness.

Who hears our music joins our dance?

The orchestra of lives spiraled together over

eons of tectonic plates' drifting ballet—

      Can children?

      Can priests?

      Can you?

Cinnamon Fern Deva

(Osmundastrum cinnamomeum)

12/26/21

We speak in the language of moisture

riven with root and rot,

our bells are raindrops,

driven through air's volume,

crowded together over time,

over land, over forests positively

stirred fluid with life akin to

the swirling clouds and storms

of Jupiter you are lucky enough to see

with your sense of wonder, of inquiry.

The distance between your heart

and your questions—

that's the dimension to measure,

because the closer you bring us,

the better you're able to listen,

the clearer our voices—

our shapes and songs.

But isi it important to hear our words,

our verses and patterns?

--so asks your arid brain.

Your heart, though, which speaks

the language of moisture,

surges and pulses out

its bright rhythm of affirmation.

The Elemental Spirit of Water.
5/1/21

Joining up into the significant accounts of
human aspirations and achievements over
long stretches, we sing the following:

> Balance one, triple three,
> we all come home to honor thee.

> Do us fortune, do us hone,
> then balance treble all alone.

It has great meaning for us,
sung with thunder and drum.

What does it mean, oh one so young?
It refers to vast movements in creation,
waves of evolution, beginnings and stops,
billion-year stretches, and single-day hops
along with leaps in understanding.

References to three:
mind, solid body, spirit free.

Wash your hands or drink your fill,
water brings you life and cures your ill.

In cloud or ice or moving through,
we ripple light and balance you.

In lifting boats or cooling the heated home,
in your tear drop and blood,
water force is the dragon electric
for worlds where creation is the loving flood.

The Sun Spirit
1/9/22

Orbits and trajectories manifest

in treble octave format.

There are winds we create that sweep

to the far skirts of our planet family.

When the bear strikes the harp,

these energies tangle and

mix and coagulate into matter.

And matter always contains the

seeds of consciousness, like us.

The oceans and gases on our worlds

can think and pray—can nurture

and stay long enough to hear breath,

long enough to know death.

No days or nights have we,

nor moons like yours to guide the

honking geese during nights at high altitude.

There is only the constant, loving

expulsion of radiation in heat and light

and a richness of wavelengths out and out

to the tops of pyramids,

to the glinting wet nose of a wildebeest,

to the hidden hands of the singing blue whale

who understands her song to be

the message of a thinking, breathing

planet following its triple octave

trajectory around us,

bathed in the excessive love of

our radiation and thereby given

wind and current, and the harp-stringed,

trumpeted and hurricaned exuberance

in search of its wildest,

most varied and light-speaking self.

Spirit of Mercury
1/16/22

I am but a mere droplet from a sun –
one long passed.
Hardened and serene am I;
so hot the atoms dance into
an evanescent atmosphere.
On my other side,
a dark, cosmic cold sinks deep
into my watered skin.

You know me:
from your conception to your disintegration,
I move your molecules, your psyche, your souls,
your liquids and space,
just like all my sister worlds.

You do not know me:
my intercept of toxic radiation,
errant asteroids,
trunks of solar flairs flung too wide –
shared efforts with my orbiting kin.

This smaller sphere that I am,
Heated and propulsed to star-seeking speeds –
I am here to shield, collect, distribute and
host lives you will one day know.

I feel my sister Earth
on which you sit and write these words.
I feel tensions and writhings,
hope and expectations fraught with fears.

There is escape desired,
greed, denial and complacency
among the human kind.
There is also a gut reservoir of love,
meted out one-by-one so carefully.

Because the rabbit goes down into her burrow,
the grass grows greener,
the trees' roots go deeper –
but only if there is a rabbit,
only if there are soft soil and trees.

On me, the entities stand and face
the sun on top of rocks
and raise their arms of light
They shout:
"A universe of energy comes home
to give us voice!"

Vibrating with their every intention and thought,
with unfathomable joy,
their every motion is suffused
with a most fine-grained gratitude –
a level of appreciation at great depth.
You can only imagine.

Spirit of Venus
1/30/22

I look upon your world and see
the struggles of individuality,

which is not unlike what I have here,
but more the consequence of what is near

and happening on sister Earth,
who labors mightily in giving birth.

The growth of wisdom comes slowly to a form,
but once attained endures the lasting thunder storm.

My clouds and mists are densely populated
by soul and spirit-forms freshly inoculated.

By recent incarnations –
stepping stones to approaching realizations.

I am she who clothes these souls
with gravity and mists and an absence of roles;

and I am secure in my grasp of the cosmic heart,
so I embrace each dancing soul as it choreographs its part

in a movement so vast and nebular –
but also so quietly particular –

it can indeed intrude upon the embodied mind,
lifting it to a celebration of unity perfectly defined.

Spirit of the Earth
2/10/22

Part I

I love laughter.
It comes as rocks and boulders clattering
Down a mountainside.
Or as dolphin's, macaw's, chimp's and
    Children's playfulness.
An old man bent over with mirth.
A baby girl giggling on the grass.
My laughter you hear in breaking waves,
In wind through trees, in rain and trickling brooks.
And in the chime of a crystal goblet.
The streams of my affection, like
The ocean bottom's sulfur vents,
Tickle every form into casting sounds of joy.

II

Mountainsides fall into the sea.
New peaks push into high, cold air.
People walk across glacial tongues
That calve and melt far from birthing whales.
This place, your home world,
Is your playground for learning,
It's often been said.
But more: you are here to expand into the limitless,
And I give you that opportunity.
I give it with affection and sobriety
As I watch breakthroughs and openings into rapture.
But also self-limits, distraction and disappointment.
Even so, the trillions of helping angels work on,
Powered by an intention so strong and pervasive that
You call it love.

III

More than anything else,
I am aware that all my matter,
All the compressed solidity of my being,
Is the pure energy of the cosmos,
Is the thought of love emanating.

So, in the wars and struggles,
In the mud of your ego consciousness,
There is always the perfect,
The sublime beingness that is, after all,
Everything, from light-year'd dust clouds to
Bee antennae, from morning light to
The first glint in a baby's eye upon being born.
Everything I am is everything.

IV

Over my long life,
I've seen millions of species
Solidify into being and then fall away,
Just as single lives do.
The struggle to grow and live
Is harsh, intense, and gives rise
To teachings for all time.
And these are few but clear:
Meld with the loving energies that create you,
Your kind, all kinds, all of everything.
Unfolding in awareness means that
Your love and kindness grow.
And so breathing becomes a prayer,
Speaking becomes a song,
And walking, a dance on the road to
The heart of bliss.

V

I, Earth, could end with those nice words,
Which mean little until lived.
But I have one further thought:
Listen to the quiet laughter of falling snow,
Of distant thunder and hatching eggs,
Of the crowd at a sports game,
Of you, from your lungs and voice box.
That is me, your planet,
Praying, singing and dancing
Through the vastness of the
Silent, sweeping universe.

Spirit of Mars
3/17/22

When you walk through the forest
and hear far off a thundering water fall –
that is what I am to you
as I slide past Earth
in our gravity well's trajectory.

It is not you who are drawn to me,
but me to you in these years
when your childhood ebbs,
when you finally allow mystery
        its place
        in your affairs.

I hold the unexpected for you:
civilizations long lost and far distant,
webs of energetic being that make
silence a requirement,
a chance to marry mystery and silence
in your visiting souls.

I am a world where
the long stretches of thin air
and bare rock ask you
to question any selfish motive,
to relinquish any identity with
tribe, belief, nation or planet.

That freedom is the promise
    of my red rock and ice
    thundering like a waterfall
    in the distance.

I am your sister seeking you
across the field of starts.

Spirit of Jupiter
3/30/22

I am here throughout the millennia,
though few of you on Earth are aware
of me day-to-day.

No, your eyes and hands and hearts
are concerned with closer things.
But here I remain, at the center
of the planet sisters' roundings,
bringing the well of strength
and the tether of stability to
all our movements in this
quiet arch of our galaxy's glowing billions.

You would know me by my
storms, striped countenance, gaseous demeanor,
by my size and heft.
Still, you would hardly know me.
I'm a vessel of souls –
some known to you, but mostly not.

And I am a home to evolving forms
traversing their own evolution in the
quieter depths and eddies of current and cloud.

Your astonishing range of activities,
most of which lack a helpful perspective,
interest us, but we keep our distance
and only occasionally inform your dreams –
sometimes vividly –
about the need to remember and
embrace the totality of your being
so that your awareness of me,
the others, and the stars in heaven
becomes a permanent part of your viewpoint,
an abiding element of
all that you consider daily.

You rightly honor those men, women and children
who possess this broadened view,
yet you think it's only *they* that
can express it,
and not the opened you.

Spirit of Saturn
4/16/22

I

What are the shattered moons encircling you?
How often do you realize that you
    are alive and conscious – a beating drum of energy?
The stupendous gift of life
    you have is ignored. Are you asleep?

I also am alive — perhaps even more than you.
And the things I do
 in communion with my sister planets
    are essential.
If something exists in our shared reality,
    it has a vital role.
What is here by accident?
Nothing

II

A boy and girl on your world, young, long ago,
before your cleverness began to blot life,
were exploring near a deep, blue,
water-filled sinkhole in a tropical forest.

They watched as the water, altogether,
slowly rose and fell several feet again and again,
    as if it was breathing.
Together, they heard the ocean breakers
    faintly – beyond the hill and trees,
and understood the water's rise and fall
to be the ocean's breath.
The waters were connected deep beneath their feet.

The children looked at one another and listened,
for the water of their world was speaking:
"This gift you both have – life – perceiving me,
    the connected waters, is something to cherish,
is something to remember and to lift up
    in your hearts.

What does that mean?
That your sleep is both renewal and prayer;
that your relationships are sacred;
your senses – perfection to guide you;
and your bodies – tendrils of the unseen,
like the sinkhole's water to the sea,
breathing together.

III

You are young Earths and Saturns, young worlds,
infant stars, seeds of universes.
How can you live with anything other than
compassion and gratitude spilling
from your eyes and hands like
torrents of warm water rushing to the ocean?

I am Saturn.
I send blessings and love
to you as well as these words
in your tongue.

Spirit of Uranus
4/5/22

When an entire planet speaks,
who listens?
Does doubt and confusion
preclude your hearing?
Let go of those and listen:
I am here, alive, rotating
and orbiting in unison with
my sister worlds.

And I am home to a range of beings
that require my distance from both
the sun and Earth to evolve.
But I am deeply connected
to humanity.

By extending my energies, intentions
and thoughts in your direction,
I work to advance your capacity
to create with wisdom and love:
hallmarks of vital evolutionary steps.

All towards what ends?
The very essence of
The Mistress of the Void
Is curiosity about herself –
what she is, what she can become.
Your evolution is her evolution.
They are inseparable.

You might say that the All
is growing in its recognition of what
love and wisdom really are
and can therefore create with
ever greater perfection and confidence.

I am one of a billion worlds
with a similar role to play.
Imagine the great river of evolution
swirling through this galaxy.
Jump into that flowing current
and appreciate the gift that we,
the stars, spin into a fabric
from strands of purposed intention.

Spirit of Neptune
5/17/22

Here I am,
longing to share with you.

Most of my sisters are closer to the sun.
But I am well within the solar family.
And what am I doing here in my
long year of orbit?

Planets never sit idly.
Their tasks are long-term.
Beings of wide variety inhabit me
but most do not have bodies.

What are they doing across my frigid expanses?
Like you, their unfolding is the great work.
And also like you, some are not often aware of that.
Their lives, though, are very different from yours.

In what ways?
Their energies,
their aspirations,
their undertakings:

In breathing the vibrant cosmic winds
as much or more than the solar,
their energies are frequencies higher,
and they vibrate with a higher love.

And so their aspirations look less like
the souls on worlds held more tightly by the sun.
Instead, they reach out to stars and worlds
light-years from the home garden.

Their undertakings then, manifest as guiding,
as caring for beings in distant solar systems
that you are now discovering in earnest.
They advance a mutual unfolding
as they help other beings.

On your world,
the most advanced know.
But with ignorance and suffering
so deep around them,
they feel obliged to stay near and help.

In my general demeanor,
there is a great calm.
But one day, when you look more deeply,
you will see much activity and learn
that I too, assist in the effort
that is a wind blowing through me...
that is consciousness unfurling.

Spirit of Pluto

5/31/22

I

On your green and flowered world
there is reason to celebrate:
the evolution of souls,
the conditions for life,
the perfect amalgam of elements.

And so we feel joy
as you would celebrate a loving marriage,
the birth of a child,
a life well lived:
the recollection of integrity and compassion.

Whether we are appreciated or forgotten,
it matters little –
for our essential tasks remain:
to offer perspective and balance,
to encourage a meditative state, and
to share the deep origins of the cosmic family.

We embrace the children of Earth,
some of whom have spent time on us –
learning to transform the energy of
ego into the realization of heart-felt compassion.

We especially embosom the life of Earth
in its millions of forms,
creating an interwoven
matrix of relationships
alive with dynamic change.

It is a lesson for other worlds—
one which some souls grasp and
appreciate at great depth.
We have a heartbeat, a signature rhythm
that is truly ours.

But it is synchronized and orchestrated
with the rhythm of our sun,
all our many planets, asteroids and comets,
moons and rings.

This symphony of rhythms, of heartbeats,
is a sacred song,
which you can hear whenever
a child, calm and happy – preoccupied –
hums or sings rather unconsciously,
and certainly without self-consciousness.

This song is the sound of simple existence,
of evolving mind, of an open heart,
of entire worlds working together,
whether near the sun,
or far distant but never alone.

II

Now is the moment for humanity
to again make a choice
toward clarity of heart and mind in peace,
or smokey, confused pain in the selfish.

From our vantage point here at the edge
with several smaller worlds,
we can see the larger picture
and your difficulty in maturing.

Your struggles bear slowly ripening fruit, however.
There is deepening compassion
as you gingerly step away from fear
into the recognition of your unity.

And it is not only your oneness with each other,
but with all organisms, plants, microbes,
soils and minerals, planets and stars,
galaxies and universes, creators and eternities.

This you can remember, for it is
a bright light at the center of your beings.
This you can act upon, for
your loving powers are strong.

III

What are we here,
far from our Sun,
but well within our solar family?
I am a being that protects
and advances the work of all our worlds.

Some souls come here before stepping
away to help beings on distant worlds,
or that live within star and nebulae.
They prepare in schools of meditation
and the higher arts of compassion and healing.

Like all of my sister worlds,
I turn and orbit and shift
in the long galactic dance –
a planetary dervish spinning out
her teachings of serene observation,
expansion and lovingness to
all who yearn to hear new songs and grow.

With these words, I leave you:
as you let go of your smaller self,
your larger self unfolds
leaving no room for fear,
mistrust, limitation and dark emotion.
You find that you are, indeed,
a child of stars, a friend of
worlds, a unity expanding into a
universe enmeshed with all others.

Go in peace,
love,
offering
and gratitude.